AN INCOMPLETE LIST OF NAMES

THE NATIONAL POETRY SERIES

The National Poetry Series was founded in 1978 to ensure the publication of five poetry books annually through five participating publishers. Publication is funded annually by the Lannan Foundation, Amazon Literary Partnership, Barnes & Noble, the Poetry Foundation, the PG Family Foundation and the Betsy Community Fund, Joan Bingham, Mariana Cook, Stephen Graham, Juliet Lea Hillman Simonds, William Kistler, Jeffrey Ravetch, Laura Baudo Sillerman, and Margaret Thornton. For a complete listing of generous contributors to the National Poetry Series, please visit www.nationalpoetryseries.org.

2019 COMPETITION WINNERS

An Incomplete List of Names by Michael Torres
Chosen by Raquel Salas Rivera for Beacon Press

Thrown in the Throat by Benjamin Garcia
Chosen by Kazim Ali for Milkweed Editions

Fractal Shores by Diane Louie
Chosen by Sherod Santos
for University of Georgia Press

Field Music by Alexandria Hall
Chosen by Rosanna Warren for Ecco

Little Big Bully by Heid Erdrich
Chosen by Amy Gerstler for Penguin Books

AN INCOMPLETE LIST OF NAMES

POEMS

MICHAEL TORRES

BEACON PRESS
BOSTON

BEACON PRESS
Boston, Massachusetts
www.beacon.org

Beacon Press books
are published under the auspices of
the Unitarian Universalist Association of Congregations.

23 22 21 20   8 7 6 5 4 3 2 1

This book is printed on acid-free paper
that meets the uncoated paper ANSI/NISO
specifications for permanence as revised in 1992.

Text design by Michael Starkman
at Wilsted & Taylor Publishing Services

Library of Congress Cataloging-in-Publication Data

Names: Torres, Michael, author.
Title: An incomplete list of names : poems / Michael Torres.
Description: Boston : Beacon Press, [2020] | Series: The national
    poetry series
Identifiers: LCCN 2020011345 (print) | LCCN 2020011346 (ebook) | ISBN
    9780807046746 (trade paperback ; acid-free paper) | ISBN 9780807046784
    (ebook)
Subjects: LCGFT: Poetry.
Classification: LCC PS3620.O5898 I53 2020 (print) | LCC PS3620.O5898
    (ebook) | DDC 811/.6—dc23
LC record available at https://lccn.loc.gov/2020011345
LC ebook record available at https://lccn.loc.gov/2020011346

For my homies, who were there.

All we are is representation, what we are & are not,
Clear & then going dark again . . .

—LARRY LEVIS

CONTENTS

FOREWORD

This is that book. It is a halo-chain of light left where lifelines
dry out, where palm meets wrist. It measures the force that
drowns out memories as it becomes a "river called History."
This is where two lives meet as men shake hands, yearning
for a passion that is not violence. Michael Torres has written
something I will be reading and rereading for years to come.
I will accidentally carry it in my bookbag to the protest and fear
losing it as I run from the forces of erasure. I will fold it too many
times and regret the frayed edges. I mean, have you read it?
Do you know Michael Torres? Have you read *An Incomplete
List of Names*?

When I recommend it, will I mention that the metaphors are so
precise they make me feel at home, even when I'm already here,
in Puerto Rico? Maybe I will say the masculinity in these poems
is as an ever-winding tenderness, that it touches itself through
distancing, forever trying to find out how much is house and how
much is labyrinth. Torres writes: "All my heroes are my homeboys
who move/ through the impermanence of their day." These
poems remind me that impermanence is a lifescape, not just a
way of being in relation to History. Those of us who write despite
this impermanence often do so in order to pay homage to
homeboys, grandfathers, Pachucos, and the selves we risk losing
through survival. It refuses to stylize loss, even as it embraces
poetry as a dangerous kind of beauty.

Whatever words I offer in favor of this book will always
fall short of reading it for the first, third, or fifth time. It begins
listing the interminable—street names, names of friends, family,
schools, words no longer in use, entire communities—but by
establishing its open-endedness, it also signals that the space
between those names is populated by the unnamable. It is
an incomplete list of names and a list of incomplete names.
It embraces that its conditions of possibility are based on
the impossible task of naming a moment, an encounter, an
intensity, a system of affects, or a chain of recurrent dreams.
Its power lies in its desire for and refusal of completion.
And yet, when I recommend it, will I mention that it feels
complete, that I feel complete, even when it is not my book,
even when it is not my wholeness to claim?

Raquel Salas Rivera

AN INCOMPLETE LIST OF NAMES

DOING DONUTS IN AN
'87 MUSTANG 5.0,
AFTER MY HOMIE CHRIS
GETS BROKEN UP WITH

I want to argue for the stars but I find them missing
through this window splattered with mud. Tonight,
I sit shotty and do not ask Chris if he's okay. This is
the kind of loyalty I know—how the Mustang
makes eights across a soccer field. I run my hand
over pennies Pepsi-ed to the center console. That photo
of his ex still blocks the speedometer and the next
few years of his life have already begun to carve
a cave. I pluck pennies into my palm. It doesn't
take long for this story to burn through the field.
The safety belt shocks my collar. Chris turns and aims
for a gate without easing off the gas. I yell *Fuck it*
to whatever I can't hear him say. And isn't that why
I'm here?—to watch chain-links swell in his headlights.
I disappear the pennies with my fist.

ALL-AMERICAN MEXICAN

I don't know if I made these knuckles
for nothing. They came from home, from
a body bounced off the hood of a Chevy
Cobalt. We couldn't turn away. Knuckles
from big brothers asking why you flinched.
You scared or what? Grunted knuckles.
Junior's rattled heart. Knuckles fashioned
from boxing gyms. Air thick with sweat.
Our wrapped hands and a jump rope. The
owner's son, Mikey, and his quick hands.
His Golden Gloves getting us to run miles,
to dance along the ropes. In through your
nose, out through your mouth. Like that.
Knuckles for when we danced with girls
whose boyfriends found us at the house
party, ready for the gasp of those gathered.
An echo of bodies bound for out. When I
left, I didn't say goodbye to any of this.

When I left, the homies told me they loved
me. And I loved them, even though when we
said it, we chased our *I love you*s with
laughter the way you cage the air
to catch a butterfly. You can't be too sure

who's listening. This is the kind of cocoon
each of us floated from. We like to be more
bee sting than butterfly, anyway. This story
was never going to be about the homie who

got out the hood with his right hook. There
was no college scholarship. I don't like the
word *adversity* as much as I think I should.
It takes up too many angles, reminds me
of standardized testing. How much do
you think about where I come from? If you
imagine where I come from. Please proceed
down the block. Absence is not wind .

through a window but the bothered walls
of a flame. Do you see, in that light, the
plastic chair my father left under an apple
tree he planted the day I was born? That's the
story I'm always moving toward

but right now, I'm on a couch at
the professor's house. And there are two

of me. One sits, legs crossed, a glass of wine
in his hand. I don't know what kind.

He offered and I said, *Sure, that'd be
delightful.* Right now, there's a podcast

I think he'd be interested in. I've been
designing my life around being the person

who says *Suffice to say...* The professor
makes a joke. My laughter surrounds me.

The other me floats between the professor
and the glass, not wondering what this man

thinks of my use of the word *dichotomy*. Did
I say it right? I'm well, thank you. I'm good

at being American: I

> clean up after my dog. I follow the paved path
> on runs. Sweat inside expensive sneakers.
> I'm a great neighbor, even on morning strolls
> where I forget my ID and must worry about
>
> police who need to make sure everyone is
> who they say they are. And if I can't confirm
> myself, what do I become? My *University of*
> hoodie. Just the hoodie? My jaw, my body's
>
> angles? *Where you from, homie?* I've always
> had the ability to vanish. It can happen like
> that. How much do words like *dichotomy*
> weigh in a mouth like mine? And if I go,
>
> my wife won't know what happened until
> the news flashes a photo where I'm bald and
> not smiling. I can fit their description. Sure,
> delightful. But not this morning, this

morning, without ID, I'm alive to witness
branches hop with birds. Even when
there aren't any birds. Some call it wind. If
you ask me. I watch the sky. *I'm good, my
G.* I can't stop

thinking of that time I saw an acrobat show
at the County Fair where a woman walked
onstage spinning plates on sticks. She
smiled as each plate wobbled without falling
and when she finished, she bowed. I stood
up to applaud at how she held it all together.

This is a plate spinning, a fan wedged
into the window of my childhood
bedroom. The foil my mother taped
over the glass. Those tiny, blurred mirrors
it held. My multiple selves. In one iteration
it's me

who spends the afternoon chasing butterflies
in his backyard. In this one, it's me who
sweeps the air. My glass jar. Boys from down
the block do not come over with questions.
And they do not laugh like their fathers.

This is not the one where I grow up down
for whatever, with the kind of tough
that grinds bones for gold dust. I don't say
fuck it if I don't mean it, the way Junior did
when the Regal came up the block
with its headlights cut. How he crossed his
arms over his chest.

Sometimes, I get tired of tightening my jaw
before bathroom mirrors, and there are days
when all I do is search

YouTube for talk show clips where
the veteran is brought home to surprise their
family, everyone reaching for each other. I
can't stop going back to the part where the
soldier appears, crisp from backstage as if
for the first time. Most often I want to be

uncategorized. One plate among many. I got
invited to dinner. If you could just give me
the   dimensions   of   this   place,   no?
The professor says, instead:

      Good night. And I want to say *Stay up* or
      Peace out. And I want the other me to unlatch

      the gate so I can be angelic in Nike Cortezes.
      A fluttered departure. No one there to ID me.

HIRED AS PROFESSIONAL
MOURNER AT FUNERAL

Soft rain over black umbrellas—that's me,
hurrying toward a huddled family. I'm late.
I fix my tie like my father did for me
during my First Communion: a knot over
his heart before placing it across mine—
something bestowed. This morning I can't
rid myself of this image, of a father
knotting his son's tie. Once, I read that actors
get themselves to tear up by focusing on
the saddest thing. The guests begin to cry. Now,
I gather the scent of Old Spice, a father
adjusting a boy's small shirt collar, the slight
whistle in his breath. We're back in the living room,
center stage. My father in black boots, his
matching belt. I am so young. I do not speak
because my father does not speak and I want
to know what this takes. Above the burial plot
this morning, clouds split the sky in half. Last time
I saw my father, years had formed since
I'd left home and the man I thought I was
supposed to be returned. We stared at the driveway

like unprepared actors waiting for someone
to feed us lines that must be said between
a father and his son. I brought up the drought;
he spoke of his lawn. Here, rain drowns all green.
The guests bid each other farewell. When I
came home, my father kicked my truck's tires,
gauging pressure, and said, *That's enough*
to the gravel, or to me. And what do you say
to that? There is something to thank him for,
I know this. But in the cemetery, my father
and I are the last ones left. Someone folds
the check into my hand while he finishes the fold
in my collar. If he kisses the top of my head,
I do not remember.

THE PACHUCO'S GRANDSON
SMOKES HIS FIRST CIGARETTE
AFTER CONTEMPLATING MASCULINITY

Just because I don't say *love*
doesn't mean it doesn't stir

inside me. I'm too young
to think it brings anything

besides problems—but it's 2AM
in the donut shop parking lot

and Diana's smoking. I don't care
for any. I sip hot cocoa, I devour

a bear claw. A night this quiet means
my homies are elsewhere, leaving me

unfolded. Diana and me, we have this
game: *If you could be anything else,*

what would it be? I've been waiting
for her. Her kissing lips blow smoke.

I've been the moon. I've been a coyote
on a hillside, howling at myself. Finally

she says, *Cactus*, and turns to exhale
away from us. *I know why*, I start

but stop. She socks me anyway, because
it's true. I imagine needles on a plant

that also blooms flowers. What men teach
boys to be, girls witness as well. We want

no one to know us. But here we are.
Diana reaches for her pack, passes me one

I decide to take. Lighter in her hand, cigarette
like a flag planted between my lips. Tonight,

what country does my body belong to?
I hear the hornblare of a distant train

neither of us can see, and I want to be it, too.
I want to be here, with her, and far away. Alone,

and unquestioned, with my homies. And if
there is a word for what it is I am, it stirs

in my gut, I assure you. Diana spins the wheel
into fire, wraps a hand around the flame.

Holds it there. What did I know
how to build except something between

myself and the world? I'll get close.
I'll stay there longer than I should,

long enough for her to see me in this light.

THE FLAME

The ballerina a boy sees spinning
      in a music box. Or in candle-

light the day of a family trip
      to Mission San Juan Bautista. The flame

of the candle, a tiny hand raised
      to stop him from watching his parents

through the window. They're yelling
      outside. Mouths wide: claws without

sound. Glass too thick, the boy too far to hear them
      this time. The candle whips after his breath.

Or, this is home. Years later. It's a music box atop
      his mother's vanity. Ballerina's silver turnkey

winding into her spine. There she is, his mother,
      gathering clothes in black bags—a background

of blurred hurry. Someone tell this boy it's okay
      to be afraid. The ballerina's arms stay raised,

curved like the tip of a flame. His mother tells him
to take only what he can carry. The ballerina's

slow spin. He wants to see what she does
when the music stops. His mother grabs his arm—

something he won't remember. He'll remember leaving
her there: a soft, boxed music clicking away;

how a flame can tremble but still hold, how quiet
her body became as she turned and turned.

MINUTES, AT THE HEALTH CLINIC

Thirty minutes since Carmen returned the clipboard
to the receptionist who watched her

the way people here flip through magazine pages
before their names are called; twenty-five since

Carmen was called. My feet rest on the faded spot
in the carpet. I notice how cold the chair's

metal armrests are. My backside's numb
on the light blue cushion but I do not move,

do not want to make a fuss. Carmen's mother sits
beside me, one chair between us. I do not look over,

afraid I'll see what her eyes say. I study
the brown door, the wood-grain pattern

and wonder when she's coming out. I wonder
about the people outside, if the same ones

will be there when we leave and know—still
shouting, still faceless, still with their

loud signs poking at the sky.
I rub the sweat on my palms away.

In half an hour Carmen will open the door
and walk through by herself with a look

she will carry years later, entering a Denny's
when we will no longer know each other.

The radio in the lobby plays "Lean on Me"
and I will not be able to listen to that song

again without remembering the click
of a wood-grain door and a woman

carefully walking through it, always
a few steps behind herself.

LEARNING TO BOX

Summer called for it. Miguel said
to his brothers: *What are you
little bitches waiting for?*—tossing

the gloves onto the front lawn.
In 8th grade, what Miguel had
I wanted: girls hovering close like kids

to a lit Christmas tree; the ability
to bloody a boy in one swing. The yard
became a ring. No bell or timer. Just us

and his brothers, yanking the gloves up
their skinny arms, lacing them
tight with their teeth, talking shit

between knots. Calling each other
putos like hocking loogies until
our mothers called us in to eat.

Juan was ten. Brian, two years younger,
and not a good listener. You know
how it goes: Brian swings like a carnival ride;

Miguel yells, *Keep your hands up*
and, *You better not cry*. That summer
I learned men are born from torn muscle tees,

sharp teeth, and pink scars on smooth faces.
There, motor oil combed over the lawn,
Bud cans crunched sunlight into silver

blades, and sweat slipped along foreheads
like commas between every other word
those boys, desperate to leave kid-dom,

spat out. We didn't want to stop. Years later,
Miguel would go to juvie for breaking
another boy's jaw. Police photos of his knuckles

and all his homies proud. Brown boys of July,
bobbing, blocking from getting bombed on.
Swift with a sharp jab. No one told us

we moved with such grace, or that passion
didn't have to be violent. Then, a long arm
through a target in the air. Brian on his back,

rising before Miguel got there first. I thought
I too could be tough enough, transfer that,
somehow, into a confidence for the girls

of high school Spanish class who knew
only the answers to last night's homework.
Once, after helping him in with groceries,

Miguel told me how, at Food-4-Less,
a condom slipped from his father's wallet
at the check-out line. How his father winked

at the cute cashier when he picked it up,
and said to his son, *Cuz you never know.*
Miguel laughed and I couldn't tell if he meant it.

What choice did I have then but to wring
laughter through my throat? That summer,
I learned laughter is a type of leaving. Maybe

that's not what we wanted. But if our mothers
called us in for dinner, we stopped hearing them.
The lights came on around us, inside each house

on our block. And we just stayed there. Laughing,
shouting, and swinging at the swelling eye
of the evening, closing it for good. Not even

our fathers, who approached the doorway
to stare with their arms crossed, but said nothing,
not even they could get us to come back in.

[MEXICAN] AMERICA

When I was a baby, Apolonio, my father's father,
would nibble my earlobe, maybe hoping to take with him
back to Mexico a small part of me.

I've been to the motherland. Well,
it was Rosarito and I was eighteen
and drunk, listening for the voice of a woman
who would dance with me. Does this count?

The older sister of a girl I wanted to date
asked if I spoke Spanish. I shrugged *kinda.*
She stared at me and my gold-plated grief.

I italicize Spanish in my poems although I hardly speak it in my
every day.
Is this forgery?

I've been walking around with an accent mark
to place over a letter like a crown.

One ear is my own, the other belongs to a man
whose name in English becomes Apollo and unfamiliar.

Two tiny photographs of my father. In one, he's all
cowboy hat and hand on the gun at his waist, somewhere
in Jalisco. In the other, he's a Desi Arnaz smile, as if to say
I told you so. Smooth hands, calluses healed, a cigarette sits
snug between fingers in a way that means he doesn't care
if it falls. Even though it's a close-up, I know
he's made it to the States.

I wonder if I'll ever dream in Spanish.

I keep the photographs of my father—one behind each ear.
Like accent marks. The father behind my own ear, a man
holding light in his hand, tells me how to get home: *find
a freeway; go east, away from water*. Behind my borrowed
ear, my father spins the gun on his finger. Wind whistles.
He tells me, when buying the newspaper, pay for one
but make sure to take two: one for yourself;
one for who you cannot be.

ON BEING **REMEK**

REMEK is a JanSport backpack stocked with Krylons. REMEK
is memory. It means a bedroom window splintered open for
fingertips to find the way back in. It's homies in black hoodies
and jeans, hopping into someone's mother's Astro van. New
York fat caps and German thin tips like dice in your hand.
REMEK of paint fumes. It's flat black and polished moonlight
stolen from the top shelf of the 99cent store. The REMEK of
adolescence, being sixteen and nodding to Tupac buzzing
through ripped speakers. It's someone turning it down to
whispershout, *Stop here. Go, Go.* It means feet grinding
gravel, feet pressed into fence. Fingers surrounding metal, it
means leaping six feet in one bound. Or getting stuck. Adidas
in the air. Prints pressed into dirt. The infamy of REMEK and
wanting to see your name on every cinderblock city wall. It's
mapping Pomona, California. The rattle and hiss of REMEK.
Spotting police by their headlights and knowing which
direction to run. Every road leads home. Morning dew on
the front lawn, and a bent window screen. It's going to bed
with a Rorschach test of spray paint on your hands and three
hours of sleep. It's looking for cotton balls and your sister's nail
polish remover before school. The REMEK of carved classroom
desks, the REMEK of dust wiped clean.

REMEK of remembrance of the many other Mexicans who
became names their fathers did not give them. Names created.
Or taken from textbooks. The end of a song. Names from the
wandering imagination, plucked like an orange—something
glowing—among the branches of the mind. Names like DIER,
MASE, and RAGE. Names like TEAL, KAON, and SIRIS.
Names that resonate in the callused palms of handshakes. This
means the only loyalty you know. REMEK of words learned but
concealed; tucked into the grooves of your knuckles where all
men keep secrets. It means knowing fear and pretending you
don't know what that means. Contents under pressure. REMEK
is memory and how the past will call back. It's not being able
to forget conflict inside names like DUSK. And when you're told
to fight, REMEK means staring at him as if you will shout in the
swinging speech of young men.

REMEK is adolescence and adolescence is knuckleheadedom.
A circle forms around the two of you and REMEK means trying
to find something to hate DUSK for—the streams of dirt on his
wrinkled shoes, the tattered cuff of his jeans—but you realize
he is more like you than he is not. And years from now you will
recall the dark face of DUSK for this reason, for having to grow
up in a town lost to potholes and dropouts, where boys take on
new names because what their fathers offered did not suffice
or could not be pronounced. Or both. The ruin of REMEK:
your friends will say—*You gonna fuck that foo up, REMEK?*—
in a way that was never meant to heed afterthought. But you
won't fuck him up. They will turn their heads at you like dogs
being whistled for. And you will lie and say: *Why? I don't
even know him.*

24

DOWN | I

By morning, all of us talked
about the boy who got shot
after school, so at recess
we found the computer lab
to look for bloodstains, a chip
somewhere in the paneling,
and stared at the opening
for long enough that it seemed
to grow larger—a tunnel
we might slip into before
escaping as men we thought
we could be. I made a fist,
not sure what to say. Miguel
said, *That foo was down for his*
shit. He asked if I was down
for my shit. I wasn't sure
what he meant but I was like,
Yeah. —Yeah? he said. *Sock me then.*
My entire body gripped.
He laughed. The bell rang. I laughed.
One boy behind another
like a row of knuckles, we
marched into class. Then out of
childhood. It took years. Later

the Lambo doors lifted when
Miguel's Accord pulled up and
a system bumping *Holler*
if ya hear me—rattled each

window. We emerged sixteen,
claiming new names on our tongues.
Some of us had cement slabs
for cheek bones. But there I was:
chubby in baggy jeans like
candlewax in the sun, soft
over the road. I couldn't
be loud enough. We looked
at the pavement, sweaty with
sunlight. Miguel said, *The streets*
are hot. The homies jumped back
in the car. I didn't want
to be left. Inside, I turned
my hat and stuck my head out
como un perro waiting
for someone to look at us
too long. It got late outside.
I yelled at the dark; my name
devoured the air. Under
streetlamps we glistened with rage.
My mother didn't want to
ask. When I got home late, paint
covered the hands strangers shook
at school the next day saying,
I saw your name up—that's down.
They wondered if I could bomb
their blackbooks; I smiled into

blank pages. I learned how to
recognize a fist before
its fingers did, how a fist
produced a handgun for some.

It was always summertime.
Mornings after gunshots, moms
gathered, tugging grandchildren,
to whisper in Spanish names
of sons until their prayers
collapsed like bones underneath
a suffering none of us
could know how to carry. They
cried in the small rooms their palms
turned out to be. Grandchildren
asked for a few dollars for
when they saw the ice cream man.

Around town, everyone wore
the dead boy on T-shirts where
he lived in a photograph:
on his bike; his hand raising
a *P*: even in death we
rep the hood. His daughter was
at the carwash fundraiser
for his funeral. She smiled
with a Super Pop. Father
pulsed against her chest—a brave
lie. So many lit candles
were placed against the fence where
he fell. A burning city.
No one could reach the sidewalk.

People in the street became
disillusion's parade.
I thought: What I know is Death
makes us neighbors again, and
that funerals look too much
like family reunions.

When the world shrank around us,
we punched walls to open it
back up. We emptied beer cans
after funerals. Danny
kept talking his shit—*Keep up*,
he yelled—until we were all
singing in Spanish. Me too.
Life was a dirge. I wanted
to go home but I was there.
Someone passed around a pack.
I was happier with smoke
waving from between my lips.

How do *you* laugh through a mask?

More names into soft dirt.
Blood kept dreaming of shadow.
More shirts with faces were made.
Into the train yard, we ran
with them. Their faces flashlights.

We washed and folded those shirts
into drawers to keep the rest
company with rose petals
humming between the Bible.

CLOTHESPINS

for my mother

I am never completely alone, especially when
on a run and grasshoppers snap into a sky resembling

the broken clothespins of childhood summers, each half
fluttering against a clear California blue, one echoing

today's, but here in Minnesota. Cloudless, I almost
believe I can take my hand and reach into it. But I can't.

What I do believe is somewhere between here and home
there's a boy in a striped red shirt, its collar loose

from pulling it over too much wavy hair too many times.
In denim jeans—ones he will grow into and out of without

remembering—he's running toward his mother.
Grass stains over his knees. Basket of laundry

she hands him as they go inside where she will teach him
how to fold his clothes, how to run a crease so that it stays.

PUSH

I. Man pushing mower

So I enter a yellow house. That's what
I've come up with. Its silence. I stare
at the floorboards. I reach a window,
and a man who looks so much like
my father I can mimic his walk, pushes
a mower. He *should* be my father
but he is a stranger, and I'm not surprised.
The house fills with the smell of cut grass
and gasoline.

II. Wanderer

Today no one forgave me. I heard the word
whitewashed and everyone knew
of my lost Spanish tongue like a ticket home
that slips under a bench. I thought about bleach
and the wrinkles of eyelids stung shut
so I began to walk the streets, listening for a way back.

Up and down blocks, the buzz of mowers.
Hedge trimmers over ivy elephants stampeding
green. Men behind machines never stopped

pushing, never stopped to turn their heads
at me or the swelling sun. I offered what
the cloudless sky offered: nothing. They loosened
bandanas from their foreheads, to swing cool again,
only to tie them back on. No one would tell me
which way to go.

III. *Street vendor*

Her frame hunched over the cart, wheels squeal
with lost strands of hair—I whistle a last chance.

She stops but doesn't look. Children swarm
with importance. Their crumpled dollars shoved

past the guilt about to leap from my mouth.
Elotes con queso, she says. She plays mother:

apron and understanding. I write down every word
like taking directions; listen to her flip back-and-forth:

tengo raspados de vanilla, blue raspberry y red cherry.
I order a snow cone; she takes my money. *Ayuda me,*

I say. She hands me a napkin and a quarter. Ignorance
is a type of penance. I know I can't go

where she is going: home to a book she will rest
on her lap before she yells across the room for quiet.

From outside the house, however, I might catch
a word, perhaps an entire phrase in Spanish

before it breaks against the closed ear of sky.

IV. *Walking through Home Depot parking lot*

I won't accept language without its love
or loyalty. Today, I found men within
thin shadows of a gas station and thought:
If I buy them bottles of water, what would
my offer offer me? Hope that they see me tender
and pliable, that they not welcome-party me
with teeth. I am so made-

-in-America. I want to believe I am still the primo
they once met, young and forgivable. But I am also
who I am by who they must be to me. Every word
we don't speak unspools in glances, silence sewn
into place. Those men against walls, laughing,
three to a circle. *Those* men. Here, everyone listens
for whistles from a truck window except me.

THE VERY SHORT STORY
OF YOUR KNUCKLES

Or the mailbox you bruised
before you left. I don't care
to trace every absence, every
avenue, until we reach what
went wrong. No. Let's start
here: the car that came for you:
a blue Civic, a passenger door's
scrape. How easy escape seems.
How an ache always asks
for a window to look out of.
Where did you see yourself?
I memorized every corner
your name covered; boneprints
on tin and timber, stamped
like lonely tracks. It was
summer, let's say 2002, yes,
the year I stopped being a boy
despite my body, despite the bike
I rode to witness the City wash
your name to puddles. I stopped
telling my mother who I was

with all night. What drowned-out
became a river called History.
No one remembered your yard.
For each street, a sheet of bleach
—reason to clip your mugshot
like wings from the Daily Bulletin.
To keep you from floating away.
You returned and the trees said *Hello*,
but couldn't tell which one of us
you were. They said, *Prove it.*
They swayed, *You can't be.* Tony,
show them your hands. Ask
the mailbox to open its mouth,
say *sorry* for knocking out a few
teeth, for buckling its knees.

TEACHING AT THE PRISON IN DECEMBER

When the evening sky loses
its blue, the dead trees blossom
                namelessness.
                We become what
         we endure.
            Today
I study maps. Routes to return me.   How odd, this necessity
my unending study
          of the past's magnitude.
Each of us carries a kind of scale.
               Once a week
I gather in a room full of men who measure
the lives they wanted
         —and still want—
by writing it down, men who do not know
they remind me of nicknames and handshakes
from back home. Despite this or because of it
                we laugh.
        We talk poetry, and do not
bring up how we got here.
           Beyond, a barbed fence carves the wind

countless. Only snow enters unquestioned—without ID,
metal detection, hand stamp—
                                parachuting through
            cyclones of razor wire.
How solemn each blade
                                must be. After class
                                                I want nothing
                        more
than to stray from my escort's side. His proper stare
and pepper spray.
            I understand this infraction.   And yet
I imagine my glove tossed
                                so that I may graze one blade
            with an index finger
                                warm and crowded
                                with my blood.

THE PACHUCO'S GRANDSON
CONSIDERS SKIPPING SCHOOL

I didn't want to be bad. But, I wanted to be bad.
Yesterday someone threw a book at the sub's head.
All I saw was a bird with paged wings. And today,

when I walked into class baggy-jeaned, he took roll
but didn't call my name. That's how I knew
I didn't have to answer no more. I became absence

in my seat, asleep; became block letters
for the name my homie bestowed. I dreamt
chain-links and angel wings—how to escape.

At some point we were awake, yes, all the brown boys
like me, and we carved our new names into desks
in the shape of hearts. What a beautiful beating.

We cut the tongues from our old shoes
to stuff into new ones later, so they'd pop
like a bullfrog puffs when it's in danger. No one

to recognize us. We were more mustache than
our mothers could manage. Before 5th period, some left.
Through a window, my homies clicked chins *Wassup*

for me to come through. Don't let the wind between
branches fool you, their eyes said. Every looking out
also implies enclosure. Out there, where I could be

anything, I placed a silver chain around my neck
and it fit like a slipped halo.

BECAUSE MY BROTHER KNOWS WHY IT'S CALLED *COUNTY BLUES,* BUT WON'T TELL ME

When my brother was taken away, I painted
our room blue to make a more manageable
sky. But I didn't want this to mean anything

beyond an offering of endless daylight.
I needed something collapsible, a place
to collect quiet, for my thoughts to become

clouds, like in cartoons. Where was I? The blue
became the room; it prepared a silence of its own.
For all the trees planted in pots near the door.

All the birds deserting the sky we abandoned.
I turned volume knobs to 10. Then, blue walls
of roar. I'm not a good liar. I've been looking

for the perfect metaphor for grief all along.
I sit with this sadness every man I know shrugs
from his shoulders. I've traveled quite far,

but've only encountered a variety of distant stares;
the calls of birds no one ever sees. This is the end
everyone hates. This is a poem. But I'm not

the speaker. The speaker is the speaker. His brother
is not my brother leaving, being called to a different
sky, another room, everything turning blue behind him.

AFTER JOSÉ CLEMENTE OROZCO'S
MAN OF FIRE

One evening the summer sun isn't enough.
Fourteen years old, a blue plastic kiddie pool

in the middle of the street. We choke a bottle
of lighter fluid over it. We strike matches

and let them fall. We ollie over
the flames. We stop to watch it melt.

From a porch, someone's father yells
with a voice as strong as his hands.

Eventually, the fire is put out. Eventually,
we each walk home and enter rooms

we will sneak out of at night to make
the best decisions and the worst. Eventually,

every summer ends and we move away.
Some of us go north, promising to return.

The rest of us rent rooms up the street,
stay close to our fathers who will, by then,

be bound to an illness we imagine, somehow,
finding cures for. Watch the slow extinguishing

of the body: Fathers with canes. Fathers pushing
walkers. Finally, fathers up the slants of sidewalks

in electric wheelchairs. And when we see each other
on the street, neither of us will have the courage

to wave. Dumb and tough is what we were.
What does that do for me now?

If I try taking it back, I imagine the blue plastic
burned into street. It's the next day: I'm already

too late. But knowing what becomes of us
and our fathers, I want to believe I can reconfigure

the sky and align its stars. The blue won't be
chipped away and, still, I circle it like an angel

who has yet to realize he's fallen.

DOWN | II

We had fun trying to die,
swerving in my Corolla,
pulling the E-brake after
the rain. I said to Danny:
*I can't see what twenty-five
looks like.* He turned and said: *Don't
talk like that.* We knew the cost
of the briefest tenderness.
On the way home, we witnessed

some foo wearing the wrong hat.
He looked at us. Danny said:
Turn back around. He jumped out.
I drove around the block while
Danny swung his fist, his whole
body at the boy. Both pushed
against the fence like a bridge
swaying. The street began its
collapse. I came back scraping
the sidewalk. Danny hopped in
breathing heavy and happy.
Who was that? In the rearview

nothing was there but the street,
the cracked way we left it.

I couldn't sleep and mornings
I saw viejos walk to Tom's
for breakfast in suits looking
like the ones they'd be buried
in. When I asked, they couldn't
tell me the names of their kids
without searching through prayer
boxes gathering above.
Suffering was a numbness.
When I didn't want to be
REMEK anymore, Dad said:
What about wanting to work?

And at the fabrica I couldn't
do anything right. Couldn't
paint, couldn't sand, couldn't speak
Spanish. Everyone there laughed—
sawdust plumed from their large throats.
I went from department to
department, fucking up. Noon,
I walked home to the memory
of laughter like a wave of
birds squawking. I counted all
the clouds. Still, every morning
the temp agency called, asked
are you free today? I was

a maintenance technician,
a plumber's apprentice. Once,
I worked with a magician
who told stories with his hands
the way homeboys threw their signs.
The sun: a palm, fingers out.
The moon: a fist. I mastered
midnight. Later, I sold cars.
You bought a Dodge Neon with
zero down. No one paid me
to count each cloud but I did
anyway. Briefly, I was
a mathematician who
failed to find a formula
for those lost years I'm sure we
made it through. I was a sleep
-deprived participant for
a college study. I was
my body's receptionist.
I wrote gospel music, then
became a carnie. Mornings,
I greased the Tilt-A-Whirl seats,
paid with free admission to
the "Saddest Man in the World
Show." When I drew the curtain,
there was someone as tired
as me to meet. He stood up
and a small pair of wings slept
against his back—a broken

heart made of feathers. I shined
turquoise for a month. That was
my favorite. No one knew
my name; it was wonderful.
I refereed boxing nights.
Men without wives waved money.
I was a secretary
for the temp agency. Once,
someone didn't say hello
but picked up. I whispered script.
It took me two weeks to see
I'd been calling my number.
Carefully, I spoke into
the phone: *Are you free today?*

[WHITE] AMERICA

No one calls me Miguel
except those who don't know me
or those who do.

America what do you want me to say?
There are too many of your voices in my ear;
I don't know what you look like anymore.
America what size are you now?
And where did all the fire trucks go with those Dalmatians
and their ears flapping like flags in the wind?
Everyone's inside the house and I'm here on the dead lawn
waiting for an explanation. Was it just a parade?—a movie?

America I keep wandering into the Hispanic section of your
                                        grocery stores.
It's a trap for us all;
I see your dream is bilingual now.
I too want a chance to refinance.
America I'm not really free, am I?
I wrote that last line to start a fire.
What I mean is, I don't believe men with ladders are coming to
                                        save me.

What I mean is, I'm fooled by sirens bouncing louder up the
                                                              block.
Nothing but police setting up checkpoints. I'm stuck watching
cops trap neighbors without papers, placing them in the firm
                                                              backhand
of patrol cars to be taken back across. I count my lucky stars
                                                   and they break
into shards in my grip.

America I don't think you have the right answers
but you speak loud.
America what do you see when you see me?
America this is what I understand: one summer,
        mowing lawns with men who'd never collect
        Social Security income, and the afternoon
        a white homeowner came out to tell us
        to trim the hedges lower, flattening her English words
        like dough with a rolling pin.
Her voice loud. I reiterated, and she asked me if I

speak English. America

I've fastened my father's machine to the truck.
The blades have been wiped clean. I'm washing
the calluses on my hands with lemon-soap and salt.
So they'll be smooth.
So no one will hear me coming.

MY BROTHER IS ASKING FOR STAMPS

And photos. Photos of me and my
new wife. He's asking for pictures
from the wedding. He's very sorry
he couldn't make it. He can't wait
to meet her. My brother is asking
if I can call a warehouse office
in Albuquerque and tell them Ray
(his cellie) is fine, and that Ray
would like his old job back, one day,
if possible. My brother is asking
for paper, asking for postage stamps,
a few dollars on his JPay. It's June,
it's July. He says it's not so bad
in here, says he's not getting institutionalized,
won't get institutionalized, not like
the others. He has TV. He reads. A lot.
My brother is asking for book 5, 6, or 12
of the *Women's Murder Club Series*.
It's May. It's March. It's May. It's October.
Happy Halloween, brother. He's asking,
again, for postage stamps, telling me
he might be programmed, sure, but

who isn't? We all need routine; he says
that one time, after chow, they let
the guys stay out a little longer
and the guys looked at each other like
why aren't we being locked down yet?
My brother says he's a confused mouse
sometimes. Sometimes he won't go out
for rec, can't stand the fact that it's going
to end. It's June. It's July. Happy Birthday,
brother. My brother is asking for stamps,
he's ending every letter with a cartoon
of himself, all homeboy-ed out,
even though he wasn't like that before.
It's like he's grown an extra life in there
and the him I grew up with is closed
until not-this August. I know I shouldn't
imagine him this way. But I will always be
younger and looking up. That's my brother,
he's asking for stamps.
                              Outside, the leaves
have turned without notice. It's the week
when every walnut seems to be falling
from the sky, and when I drive home
I run as many over as possible. It's June.
Happy Birthday. It's November. My brother
says he'll write when he can, he knows
I'm busy. Everyone's busy. It's August.
It's August, and he's looking for stamps.

ALL-AMERICAN MEXICAN

Here's a small story about the sky. It's yours,
if you want it. I'll leave it right here.
It's the size of a 2016 Toyota Corolla
windshield and begins with a song
on the radio, the name of which I forgot
to write down. I was too busy

being someone better in my mind. It was
summer there. A river, a raft. Excuse me
for making this story about myself. This isn't
what I'd planned. Through the windshield,
clouds formed over the prairie and chopped

the song into static. Bits of gray-black clung
to the air. The song ended and I turned down
the radio. Clouds so dark and heavy with rain,
it seemed a task for them to hover.
They resisted, like eyelids, to stay awake.

I know a man who'll never begin his novel
because he hasn't gathered enough data.
He obsesses over weather. He asks me how

much I trust the rain. With his fists, he
shows me what a cloud is willing to do.
How it will

reject its weight. All of it. And suddenly.
It has no choice, really. And the wind?—
has nowhere to go but with the water
it carries. *It'll take trees with it. Kids'*
bicycles, your shadow, if you're not careful.
Imagine:

an Olympic-sized pool coming down on you.
It can take a commercial jet, he says, *right*
from the sky. His list of feeble objects takes
days to say. It's as if he's sure I'll forget
once I walk away.

Only I don't. I remember each item and plan
to build a bomb shelter, a suit of armor. I want

to live longer. I stop eating red meat. I call
my father and tell him I love him and say I'm

sorry, though not for what. I buy a golden
retriever, research how to stimulate neurons.

Anything to keep me from ruining. Because
I wanted to age with grace, I became

a poet. It made sense. Truly. I could not see
myself age into, say, boxing: stepping into

the ring, weak and sleepy. With a cane. But
in poetry, I saw a casket to ease my failing

bones into. At a Halloween party my first
year in Minnesota, I walked into a house
where people I did not know chatted away in
small circles. I walked, dressed in the gauze
it took me an hour to wrap myself in. I wanted
to be invisible or unliving. Or both. I met a
woman and told her about California. When
I mentioned *my homies*, she laughed. I stared.
She stopped and said, *Oh, you're serious.*

Later, a shirtless man in a mask held up a
Styrofoam sword and asked if me and my
homie/white friend were a couple. Through
his eyeholes, he followed my tired arm over
Brad's shoulders. I paused. I said, *We're just
a couple. Of guys. Drinking beers.*
He laughed. I did too. But it was more exhale
than elation. His Styrofoam sword shook
as he walked away into a cloud of his own
laughter, which hovered over me.

Laughter fell across our shoulders like rain.
The sort of which you can't move through.
An Olympic-sized pool of funny. A thicket

of drunken bodies swayed. They watched
me. I tried to go on unnoticed and American.
Beer pong and bad jokes. Isn't that it? Isn't
that a way to disappear? But they did not
know who I was, where I was from, or what
brought me here. I had to explain what they
were seeing. They pinched and picked at my
bandages. I came loose and held a heap of
gauze guts, put it to my nose. To remember
who I was. They laughed. Then a laugh
track played throughout the house and I
knew everyone was watching. I bundled my
bandages and found the door. It was that
simple. At least I believed it to be, and so,
for a while, it was.

Onstage, I tell the audience where I grew up,
what that means. I point to my chest. That's
what poets do. Somehow, we end up at
Love. Every time. How it fails, how it saves.

Who it belongs to, after all. When it's over,
someone approaches and thanks me for *my
story*. There is nothing to say to that so they
continue with how glad they are

I turned out alright, *growing up the way I
did*. This is how you become an artifact with
ears. This is what I've come to warn you
about. I'm just a poet who knew he couldn't

put the gloves on forever, who knew, one
day, he'd be too tired to lace up and would
only want to ease his body into a small,
closed-off space. I walked home

from that Halloween unraveled. Leaking
gauze that led back to the party.

Under every streetlight, I did not talk to my
shadow. I did not ask how it was doing.

Don't mind this suffering. There's not much
to see here, anyway. But if you must, if you
absolutely must look, please do so in an
orderly fashion. The line starts right over
there. Keep your voices to a whisper.
Whoever gets used to this sadness first, wins.

Because I am a poet, I carry a notepad in my
back pocket for when I am alone or because
I'm sure to forget. Once, back in California,

my homie saw me pull the pad out, and
called me the Sensitive Poet. Therefore, I
was. It doesn't surprise me now, how easily

I come apart. But around the guys, he traced
a tear down his cheek. My homies chuckled
with their chests, all muscle tee and tattoo.

I did not mind. Not for a long time. A cloud
is only a room that fills and fills. Then a door
opens, everything barreling out.

I never retrieved the gauze. I've made maps
like this all over the country.

I have a confession to make. I am more
mummy than I thought, something gone,
ghost perhaps. Something you find in a room
gone dark. Are you there, wind?—it's me,
Michael. What I mean is, sometimes I don't
have to be my homie's homie. I can be no one
to those foos. I am so far away, here, in
Minnesota, so small and unraveled
nowadays. I am not what they remember.
I see it in their eyeholes. Somehow, I am less.
And when I say homies, I'm talking about
those south-side-Pomona homies; right-by-
the-60-freeway homies; down-the-block-
from-Tom's-burger-and-across-the-street-
from-where-Nacho-Moreno-got-hit-by-
a-car-on-his-way-to-8th-grade-one-morning
homies. By where Nacho's shoes flew off.
And we joked about size 10 Pumas growling
through the intersection. That's fucked up.
Right there is where I grew up. That driveway
and sidewalk where my homies parked.
The homies I'm trying to tell you about. I'm
leaning into an apology. Trust me, I'm a poet.
There's always something to reach back for.

I got this list of people I hate that I don't
know what to do with. It grows and grows

like a cloud carrying rain and all I have
are their names and what they did. I fold those

pages into my back pocket. Right next to my
notepad where all the unwritten poems gather

when I cannot sleep. I lean to the right
because of these people I hate, because of

these poems I can't finish. When I sit,
I always think I'm going to fall over but

I don't. I'm still here.

       Fuck your butterflies, your lilacs and sunsets.
       Fuck your hillsides, your candlelight of fear.

I'm building my own country. It looks like
my 7-year-old self, rocking a Looney Tunes
Raiders tee and throwing-up the Westside.
My country doesn't speak Spanish but

it knows when you're talking shit.
My country fits onto this very page.
My national anthem keeps getting remixed.
We're working on a website.

This is American-manufactured masculinity
at its finest. And yet, I am responsible

for the raised trumpets, the snapped-into
Slim Jims. I am responsible for the mutation

of the word *triumph*, for the Igloo cooler
heavy with beer bottles and an ocean of ice.

In the dream, my homies don't recognize
me. I show them my tattoos, but nothing. I
name the scars on their bodies and I tell
them where we were when it happened and
what we learned that day. Jesse takes the
longest to convince. *Remember watching
Knight Rider? After school, every day, for
2 months. Until the doctors left a grave of
staples from where they pulled the screws.*

This morning, thunder woke me and I knew
it was only God. This doubt, it is so
American. Still, I walked outside. Of course,

all the neighbors were there in their bright
parkas. Fools. I wore my armor, ready. We
tilted our heads and kept our eyes open

for the heaviest rain. Gray-black clouds
paraded the sky but did not speak. Far off into
the western distance, where it was still night,

flashes of light showed us the valley's teeth.
We turned away knowing it was useless. At
the door, I could smell coffee, but understood

it was only my memory of coffee, something
I wrote down once, something I added next to
a list I don't know how to finish.

SUSPENDED FROM SCHOOL, THE PACHUCO'S GRANDSON WATCHES *HAPPY DAYS* WHILE HIS HOMIE FULFILLS PROPHECY

All morning I search for my grandfather
in zoot suit pants like two pairs of parentheses
in case he happens to walk into Arnold's.
But after a few episodes the whole gang
bores me. I don't know anyone like Richie
or the Fonz, who isn't as hard as he thinks.
It's that leather jacket everyone wants or fears.
All my heroes are my homeboys who move
through the impermanence of their day . . . Right now,

Mr. Appel is calling one of my homies to the front
to solve for X because he thinks it was that foo
who yelled out *Mr. Apple!* from the back of class.
My homie, who knows the answer is 7 and −7,
will trace an apple on the board before leaving
Pre-Algebra forever... My heroes are good
at their getaways and not saying goodbye.

My grandfather used to say it was all about balance:
being Mexican at home and white out there. He invented
tightrope walking and sold his secrets to the circus. Now,
I read history books. But don't say anything. They called
my grandfather Pancho, they called him Greaser.
Our achievements listed on the page nobody wanted
to print. Okay, maybe I don't know that grandfather, just

spun one into existence, a web I could rest along. I wanted
to use my head like my hands and hold something. Right now,
Richie and the gang are in trouble. Someone fucked up.
It won't last. I've seen this one. Right now, no one is
stopping my homie. I don't know if I would have.
I must remember this. Fonzie laughs and everyone joins—

I don't know why. They don't either. The credits roll.
The outro plays. My homie jumps the fence by the track,
by where the ice cream man always parks after school,
and the chain-links rattle after him.

STOP LOOKING AT MY
LAST NAME LIKE THAT

Nothing in my life was crooked or broken.
Or potholed. Not haggard or tired. Not poor
and unfortunate. Nor merely lucky. No one's
father returned from work with callused palms
every evening. No one got to where they were
in life with the help of a new-to-the-area teacher,
who stopped at nothing until our dreams came
to fruition. Please. Our parents paid for those
university tours. On weekends, we went out
like families do. The zoo, science museums.
Summers, my parents said I love you, leaving me
at camp where I earned badges spinning twigs
until sparks spilled out. In September, no one
came to class with torn or tattered clothes.
No one got beat up for being less than. Please.
Boyhood was a ballad. Our parents sang
when they bathed our brothers. No one
became what this world carved out of desperation.
When it rained, we got picked up from school.
At home, a change of clothes on our beds. Yes,
we all had our own beds. Yes, each of us had
our own room, as well. We made boats

out of egg cartons. There were no gunshots
or helicopters to stop us from sailing those ships
along the curb's current. With the world ahead,
we opened our small yellow umbrellas,
some sudden burst of sunlight to walk right into.

DOWN | III

One day you wake up. Like that.
Like stories from 2nd grade.
But you're twenty-five, knowing
you must leave. The guys ask: *Who*
do you think you are? They ask
REMEK—a boy you haven't
been in so long. But you look
cuz it takes you back across
the dry grass hill you weaved through.

Then, you recall places where
your name rests: the ditch behind
Miguel's; the train tracks after
AM/PM; this long page.
You see boyhood: cap gun and
soccer field. Free lunch and its
long line, the number you had
to memorize. Boyhood of

bullet holes, and monkey bar
laughter of girls who said you
played too rough. Look: your fists: skin

stretched over knuckles like
drums. Look: you're sixteen. Your poor
hands not knowing how to be
themselves, how to hold a face
close without imagining
it hurt. Four boys next to your
father's car. Arms crossed over
chests puffed. Chins up. No one smiles.

You were never not REMEK,
even if only a trace—
a small splintered space the shape
of a mouth broken open
or where bullets tunnel sleep.

Before I left, I wanted
to tattoo this town across
my back. I thought   POMONA
between my shoulder blades like
a pair of wings for all those
stories I had just in case
the sky asked where I'd been. Here

I am without it—tattoo
or town—on a highway in
Utah. But I can still talk

about the veteranos,
how the green tattoos on their
arms will always mean something.

Ask, and my name is Michael
but they still   call me REMEK.
I can still trace the sound of

a clicking bike chain back to
a boy who hasn't died yet,
who's about to leave this street

on a chrome GT Dyno.
This boy, with a name that could
have been my own, waves bye. Though

he doesn't have to, he does.

AFTER THE MAN WHO FOUND ME DOING BURPEES AT THE PARK SAID: "I CAN TELL YOU LEARNED THOSE ON THE INSIDE."

I came here to write you
    a story
             where four brown boys set out
to solve a murder
          in their hood.

    But my characters keep
    getting stopped
             by cops
      and told to stay
      still. All the officers ask
is if my boys have anything
sharp   that might pierce
             while they search.
                    My boys learn
                    to lace fingers
                    instead of gather
                    evidence.
        You can spend your whole life
      unraveling. Even tempered
      glass
          is meant to shatter—just
                  quietly.

(At some point, all my homies
were down for whatever
and I don't know why.)

How do we decide
which bodies are
worth defending?

All we need is one clue,
a break
in the case.

I can't finish this
story, this story I wanted
you to have. I spent

all day running
my fingers like a searchlight
over my body.
Now, I stop
to read the wrinkles
that rest over my knuckles. I'm tired.

My hands outstretched. I want it to be okay

to see my skin as a landing pad
for little birds' feet. My wrinkles

as mapped wind. I think they could
be   a boy's grid
for charting stars. Yes,
this is his
chance to give each one
a name.

ARS POETICA

In the photograph, the sun sharp across sky
covers the street behind us. It must be late
afternoon. Everyone says *hurry*. A camera
clicks. We walk away from the scene
of the crime just before security gets there
to ask if we painted those names. Of course,

the other day, the freight train's horn blared
through my window and I thought of hopped fences
and what being fifteen was like again, as if
the train's echo—the way it opened up—was
wide enough to hold all those years. But it can't.

And I can't tell you the streets where my homies
grew up. Not anymore. Not the names
of their little brothers who followed us around,
swinging branches at ivy bushes. That photo
holds us there and does not. Not really. We left

the frame and did not look back at our names
until the City had covered them. Until it was
too late. Names met with deletion.
What did we become but an echo
we called the future. And those boys in the photo

I stuck in a box with everything else I owned
and taped shut? I don't know where they are.

The morning I left, my parents held each other
in the frame of my truck's mirror and shrank
as the road opened. Miles and miles under
a widening sky that dwindled finally,
over a Midwestern apartment and a life

that turned into mine. Now, I look out a window
and I cannot go back. Not really. I have this
photograph to stare at without knowing
who we became. There is the sun. Slightly left,

fences we jumped, a wide field, its stubborn
weeds breaking through earth. A trace
of oil near tracks. Trains covered with our names,
bearing their slow, metal death in a quiet
Colorado yard we'll never see. A hiss of stars

over nothing. Once, I asked the sky what it remembers
—a type of prayer for what I could not take with me.

Tonight, all the train cars are gone. No one I grew up with
rents a room in this town. This poem has taken me
years to reach because every name on the wall,
even my own, rang out across the sky, and fell
over a field that no longer exists. Our homegirl,

who found us in the frame of the disposable,
who we hurried, pretending not to care, says,
Okay, I'm done and means it. She moves, marries,
makes a home somewhere in Arizona. Echoes. Listen

to my steps across the hardwood—a sound
that adopts the air it moves through, that decays
behind me. It rents a room in my mind. This
could be a moment to measure distance with.
This isn't a poem. It's a history book. Recorded

with Krylon, buffed out by City employees
who were just doing their jobs. Wall after wall
like pages we kept leaving our names on. The color
of loss, a flat black or something close. I've never been
as precise as a blade of light. Those homies
under the sun. They're more phantom than for real.

My homies, I mean. There must be someone better
for this job than me. Outside my window, the street
melts into a quiet that tells me I'm not the only one

who forgets. I want to ask God what kind of gathering
this is. And why.
                 If there is a home for me to go back to,
I'm not sure I know how to get there.

MY HOMETOWN AS A MAN
RIDING A BICYCLE WITH NO CHAIN

His legs: a too-quick clock, a kind of cruel that tells me
any time away from home is too long. Pomona becomes

a man asking if I want to buy his MP3 player. He raises
headphones to my face. Listen, he says. No one believes him.

But he doesn't say about what. It's how they say yes,
but don't look. I nod. He talks about his daughter who works

at AutoZone, who's the manager now, the jefe. But his son,
who I'm certain I went to school with, who walked into 5th grade

one morning with shaved eyebrows and sat down without
saying a word, who never spoke to anyone ever again,

he does not mention. Not even once. Where have all my
classmates gone? Where I grew up has nowhere to live,

but he says he'll be alright, he'll be alright, he'll be alright
cuz the lady from next block over owes him for mowing her lawn.

And have I seen a Bible around? No one's going to pick it up,
he says, not unless it had a hundred dollars in it. Wouldn't that

be something? He's nodding, he's balancing himself
on the bike. He's trying to leave, but will I be here

tomorrow? He might be around, my town's always around.
So how about that MP3? I can keep it if I want—No,

how about for 10 bucks? My town is presenting
its callused palm. Now, my town—relentless—pedaling

like everything is alright, like everything is alright,
like a Ferris wheel no one's going to ride. Look at it

spin through the evening: each basket scooping sunlight
then shadow—the carnival worker we turn away from

calls for us. And keeps calling, long after he knows we're gone.

MY NEIGHBOR WHO KEEPS
THE DYING THINGS

From her porch, she tears red duct tape,
    binds a snapped branch to an end table. It takes
the leaves to tell us the truth. But we're better at bringing what's
    dead

    back to us. On her porch, two pumpkins—one scarred
with tiny growths like the map of a country
    that's been at war for years and another pumpkin I'd call

pretty—sit atop the table. Each existing, perhaps,
    to make fun of the other. Beside them,
a cattle skull that I can't decide is real or not.

    From this far I don't think my neighbor can see me.
But then, with a piece of tape between her teeth, she says
    Hello and then my name. The tape fixes her

against the backdrop of this late afternoon. We are all
    the dying things hoping to stay close to something more
vibrant than ourselves. Beyond her porch, the last leaves hang

in powdered yellow—sharp but easy to shake off.
This time of year the wind reminds me to call home. In October,
    it's not hard to see what I can't have anymore. Tonight,

rain will wash the sidewalks. And in the morning
    only the dark impressions of leaves will be there
to tell me: memory is first an annotation for loss.

VISITS

Thick glass between us, my brother and I each reach
for a phone receiver. Mom and Dad behind me. His voice
chipped with static. We have thirty minutes starting
seven seconds ago.

> I paint my five-year-old goddaughter's nails,
> roll gloss across her lips. Pink plastic slippers
> light when she walks. Here, she tells me, I'm
>> a prince.

My brother tells me his lawyer will be here
tomorrow. In the meantime, he reads books.

>> I read an article.
>> Tips for a Better Life.
>> 3. *Smiling*
>> releases endorphins.
>> But the mind cannot
>> distinguish a real
>>> smile
>> from a fake.

My goddaughter runs. I find her,
slide on the shoe that fits. Again.
Each time, we dance and she kisses my cheek.

>> My brother won't
>>> explain
>> how to make dice

                              out of cereal. But
                                    the guys
                              roll them, add up
                                    each turn.
                              A game called Ten
                                    Thousand.

I smile, not knowing how
to be anything other than
a little brother.

              On a plane, the world
              is so knowable. I can distill it
              to elementary geography. Clouds
              sky sun. I like to think it's this
              simple. It makes it easier to fall
              asleep in the air.
I never tell my goddaughter goodbye.
I say, *I'll see you later.* She hands me
two cookies and I leave with pink glitter
on my beard.

              On the last day of 6th grade,
              someone asked if we'd have recess
              in junior high. We all looked up
              at Mrs. Swearingen who couldn't
              put into words that we weren't
              coming back to this.
                    Our phone call ends before we finish
                    saying what we want to. I mouth *I'll write.*
                    Mom says if you flip the receiver upside down
                    and speak into the opposite end, he'll hear
your goodbye on the other side.

ELEGY WITH PUPPET STRINGS

In high school, there was a boy
who went by DIER. Out of respect,
and because he was the best
graffiti artist I knew, I never called
him by any other name. This memory
comes with the end of an afternoon
and an '87 Corolla idling by the curb,
waiting for us to go. There's no other way
you can have it.   I learned long ago
that a name can be written on anything
          and stay. DIER, for example,
holding an empty spray can, traces his name
on the sky. I still see it. And when it stays
with me long enough, there I am, again,
          at my desk in 10th grade Geometry,
hunched over ripped graph paper; the voice
of Mrs. Graham rises behind me. She yells
about the circles I can't draw with a compass.
Watch mine curl out in spirals: every small loss
          blossoms. And there's no way
to contain any of them. Not the Corolla
I had until the axle snapped, not DIER's

wrist as he practiced his name, even in class—
DIER, whose indifference for police sirens
bouncing around those nights we spent
painting, somehow calmed me too.

That was the year I was no one
and realized it. So I followed him into train yards,
rattling.

I used to believe what we left came back
like a circle—in memory. It returns, altered.

DIER and the silvers we stole
from the $.99 store. How we coughed over
the clack of marbles in cans fit against our belts
and bellies all the way out to the parking lot
where our homies waited in the Corolla in case
we had to run. A person can't stop

themselves

from thinking about who they were
or where an abandoned building,
with its boarded-up windows, that mattered
to no one except us, stood. And DIER there,
silvering his unfinished name with a focus
I likened to genius. The spiraling of his *e*,
a small, open window into another dimension,
where I could see, even then, his name at the front
of an art gallery.

And what did we know of the years
to come, of what we had to do with them? That year
I pretended not to care about school until I didn't
—swapping textbooks for paint in a JanSport.

A whole year can go like this.
                            Then a bell rings,
you get up and are gone. It happened this way
and I couldn't contain it. When I left, I forgot
to leave.   What I mean is one of me stayed
there   with DIER, who would continue
looking as young as he could no longer possibly be:
those baggy khakis; that oversized black hoodie,
as if asking *what really happened to me?*
                    There are no small losses. DIER,

I can see your wrist moving   in slow circles
across the air   just as someone honks the horn.
DIER, I say again, *the homies are waiting.* You look down

        to where the birds
have left
        the branches nodding,
and you say to me, *Why not let them?*

FROM MY CLASSROOM WINDOW AT
THE PRISON, BEFORE STUDENTS ARRIVE

Because the blinds stay open, I see birds. I watch how
men watch those birds. They monitor flight paths
and a soaring appetite for the crumbs they shouldn't've

pocketed from chow. The indifferent birds ask for nothing,
yearn for nothing, except perhaps the sky, which is nothing
to them but magnetic blue wind—their one great war

of journey. I've been thinking about mine lately. My own
great war. Once, I met a man who'd been waiting hours
for a storm to hit. At the park, he told me how difficult flight is

for birds. He stared at the humming sky and disappeared. Later
that night, I could not fall asleep. Not with a fact like that. Instead,
I sat at my coffee table and fed a dying rubber fig tree

filtered water and the eggshells I broke apart, calling them
my little countries. I thought of being president. Then I asked
myself, why can't I be king? When I arrived at the idea

of God, I began to float. When I woke, I understood
my only burden is that of a simple life of a man who can go home
and think and care for plants that do not know

he is their father. If I am no one to these leaves, to whom
do I belong? Thus, my great war is with myself. A wingspan
of stirring thoughts that ask what's next, that wait for my response

like the men beyond this window. Breadcrumbs, tiny questions
for birds. Each man tossing a piece at the air anticipates a swooping
answer, tries not to think of what goes uneaten, of what falls

toward death. Wet and certain. That patch of grass they walk,
its cold blades. It's late October. Every step stiff and speechless.

THE PACHUCO'S GRANDSON
CONSIDERS THE SILVERSUN PICKUPS' ALBUM
DIANA LENT HIM WHEN THEY LAST SPOKE
SEVEN YEARS AGO

this morning the sky stays   hidden   by the kind of gray
you like   egg carton thick   slothslow   jamming sunpath
heavy breaths of rain land   one at a time   it should be late spring
but there are no leaves   to catch what keeps   falling I am
alone of course   CD in my hand   I've been waiting
for the sky   to tell me what to do   next   my life's not
been hard   but I've spent it   all   without looking
over my shoulder   at the expanse   of dust I made   from what
I carved away from   the curb I called   kingdom   God knows
how to make a sign   out of anything   a song played on the radio
for the fifth time that day   petals plucked from flowerheads
yesterday Danny told me you   got married   he said *Diana*
got married   like that   and with the respect   or pity
men have for each other   he did not face me   I wanted him to
think this was news   as well   I didn't want to be   lonesome
nothing's news   if you pay attention   the heavy sky
rumbles   whatever   it will be has been barreling its way
here   I didn't answer Danny   didn't think I had to   but because

silence gathered   its storm   between the kind of guys we grew
to be   he said   *why you all   butthurt*   really
I was thinking of a boy I am not   a boy on a skateboard from days
                                                                                    before
pushing pavement   gripping a bouquet   of roses   did he get
                                                                                    there
to where he was going   I hope not   and I hope so   I wanted to
hate that silly   boy   but I couldn't   instead I told Danny
foo   shut the fuck up   and laughed   the sky has nothing
                                                                                    to say
this morning   and when the clouds decide   to go   the sun will
point at me   and ask if I   will stay   for more
or pay what I owe   of course I break the CD I was always going to
                                                                                    snap it gone
it doesn't play anymore   hasn't   for years   it's okay
if you know this now   I used to keep it   inside the glove box
where I knew it was   even if I didn't want it   to remind me
of those years   it did   but here   watch me bend it   I can
do it without the sky's answers   watch the light warp   like a
                                                                                    bouquet's
plastic wrap   struck by sun see   the way it fits into my fist   let me
make it   less   as long as I turn   away   right after
as long as I don't   for an hour   pluck pieces   from my palm
the way a child might   toss   daisy petals   might say something
                                                                                    about
love   as each bit hits the ground

1991

Instead, let it begin with an eyelash
      resting on fingertip—empty
teeter-totter at the park where I played
      as a child. Yes, this is memory
half made-up. Because.

Because, that time I dug into sand
      for the other side of the world
and was given a red shovel by a friend
      who I'd imagined there with me
—did it not still happen? For years,

I mistook *horticulture* for a *hoard of culture*.
      So much culture captured, I thought,
like so many shelves in a library
      that keeps needing to add rooms. One
for the history and evolution of the vicuña,
      one for what happened to paper.

Down a corridor of the mind, my mother
      sets lunch on the picnic table,
and I must clap sand from my hands
      where the maps of my life have yet
to tell me how brief I will be this light.

ALL-AMERICAN MEXICAN

All I wanted was a Cadillac on chrome, real
diamonds in my ears, and someone to call
my name through a crowd. Instead, me
and the homies drove to the mall
in my hatchback, rocking dog tags with
Tupac on 'em; we lived for his
Westside fingers. We stopped at "Nothing

but Silver," a store where I sifted through
glinting trays of jewels for princess-cut
earrings. No one asked if we needed help but

everyone stared a long time. No one called
our names so we took new ones. Swallowed
them whole and they grew inside us. Inside
the food court bathroom our new names
bloomed black from Magnum markers;
inside stalls I practiced the *R* the *E* the *M* the
E the *K*. Our names too real for us to contain.
We left and I was glad my hatchback's
bubbled-up window tint distorted our faces.
Everything is always up for interpretation.
Yesterday I ran

an image search of the white boy from 10th grade who said I looked like a dog. I wanted to find him posing in a too-wide tie for a job his face would tell me he hated.

When I found nothing, I thought he might be dead, so I looked for a park to sit with my guilt, wondering if I could've saved him, had we become friends instead, had I helped

retrieve his stack of notes blown apart by the wind. I am mostly filled with fantasies where I'm the hero: a parade and a Coupe de Ville to wave from; the Key to the City the mayor presents on a red velvet pillow.

Now, when I visit home I want to cry but the homies would notice. And it's not that they'd laugh and call me a little bitch. No. We are only as young and thuggish as America needs us to be. The problem is my homies wouldn't recognize the puzzle my body has made of itself.

Let me say it like this: I'm a stuffy June room, and the homie has only been taught to pry open whatever might test him. That's real.

Once, I was so real I became a cathedral at noon. Not the bell itself but the rope pulling sound from absence. I was only my heart

glowing against the bones holding me back.
Everyone stood to watch. Someone yelled,
Fight. Someone said I was scared. But I was

so real I burst into the wind like *Fuck
the world.*   Nothing dissolves like I do.
I came here to create a diversion, to splinter

furniture for the fire. If I'm going to be real,
I am who I've always been: a boy seeking
an orbit to align with. One day I'ma get

> *POET* tatted on my chest. Only instead of
> the *O*, I want a window through which you
> can see my childhood backyard, way before
> I became something like a souvenir.I might
> make my artist ink the tire swing. He says
> the worst it'll hurt depends on where
> I want to plant the trees.

ELEGY WITH ROLL CALL

1. *Cartography*

A heap of clothes snaked across dirt
under the freeway overpass as if fallen
off a hanger or off a body. And if it is
indeed off a body, then the body's gone
into the green city air, choking through
exhaust fumes, reappearing, as I've seen it
—him, a man under a shade tree: cardboard sign
his fingers become teeth around, bracing
words he's written. Let us call him Vanishing
Man. It might be easier to lose him this way,
if no one knows his real name.

11. *How I Remember Hands*

I used to take walks with my mother
after dinner. Those evenings, I—a boy
still—held her hand as we passed
the convalescent home. She'd tell me
to wave to a man who always sat
behind a glass door. I would, then
turn away. Then I'd look back. I think
I remember him only because I keep
wondering when I'll forget his hand
there against the glass.

III. *Graffiti Meetings*

Fridays we gathered. Homies helped carry
that old, round table to the front yard
where we set it under a tree. The rest of us
found a chair or bucket to pull up, lean in.
From our pockets: paint markers, Sharpies,
tubes of blue acrylic and waxy streaks.
We took to the table and tagged over each other,
as was custom. Someone, usually KAON
or DIER, called us to order so that we'd look up
from the fog of fumes writing our names made.

iv. *A List of What I Want to Be*
When I Grow Up, Ages 7–28

Superman. A firefighter. Football player. Lawyer.
Professional wrestler. Pro skater. Tornado chaser.
A fuckin' gangster. Alive. Sittin' on chrome. Paid. Something like Pac.
A poet. Full-time, with benefits. A good father.

v. *In an Alternate Universe*

I said, *See you next week* to Curtis, my boss, who bought
his employees Gatorade and Famous Stars from Carl's Jr.
on days that cracked triple digits because he felt guilty,
knowing they'd never collect Social Security income.
And in this universe, I continued working with those
Mexican fathers who, because they could not stop
their R's from rolling, called the boss *Curlies*
and laughed at themselves

before anyone else could. Here, I returned that following
Monday to tighten the ropes choking lawnmowers
to the truck. I hopped into a static-packed cab—
a soccer game always being played on the radio.

Sunlight forever rising over the houses
across the street. Frozen water bottles thawing
in our hands. The driver, a man I only ever knew
as Chino, yelling *GOL* every time any of us tried
to nap on the way to wherever it was we were going.

VI. *Confession*

In my attempt to escape vanishing, I left and thus
defeated my own purpose. I told friends: *I'm going
to Minnesota* because I could not say, *I can't be here.*
And not knowing the place, they could only imagine
me going into the state's large name.

                                  I'm the one
who left, so I can't say for sure what became
of those boys. I wasn't there. The further away
I am, the harder I look for home.

VII. *2003*

I don't know the names of those boys
who painted Pomona the same years I did,
not the names their mothers gave them
anyway. But I saw what they wrote, how each
moniker made a reputation that loomed so large
a garden appeared there, and in place of what proctors
and principals called our futures. It's true.
We cared for the calamity we planted,
rewriting our names each night.
                    Now that I'm gone
I ask myself if pride is what makes leaving easier?
Does rupture begin only after its realization?

VIII. *Another Confession*

We name things because we don't want them
to vanish.   Because we painted our names
over and over, certain limbs of Pomona healed
thick. Paint bubbled in the sun. Layer over layer
of proof we'd been there. So, I'm leaving you

with this: a heap of words. Names layered between
the stanzas of a poem that ends just before it rains.
Names as big as gardens. And inside each, a flowering
of nights that once mattered and, so, still do.

ix. An Incomplete List of Names

REMEK • DIER • KAON • SIRIS • D-SPERS • FALSE •

LEER • KERB • EPIK • JEMR • KRIME • DEST • DENS •

KLAS • HALOE • SPORE • SLAMO • SLICK • EWOK •

WEBS • AIMS • OASIS • D9 • TINY • PRIOR • TRACE •

EKEM • MASE • RAGE • TEAL • TIMBR • TREBO •

CEXO • CHAPARO • NANO • KROME • SHINE •

BLOOM • BASEK • GABS • MAR • JEMS • JUKE •

HALA • LILS • ASKR...RIP to CHEEKS • INNER •

PECK • TONE • TRUE • STRETCH • WAIS • GEE •

BIGGIE • GLIMPS • BREW • PHOR • ALOE • CLUE

x. The (Annotated) Six-Word Memoir

My homies
still call me
REMEK.[1]

1. It's been years. Families in tow, we bring brew, food, and fire. We present the small children we've made. Have them shake hands. Our children—for whom we will be mysteries—look up at us, then at the clouds, which escape everyone.

I emerge, dragging the old table from the backyard. The homies cheer, arms exclamation points. Beer spills from plastic cups.

We settle into seats, slide fingers across tabletop. Beneath dust, the sticky angles of lettering. Someone recalls my pant leg snagged on a fence, running from security in boxers. The fading slap of sneakers against street. Our laughter crosses out the evening. No one leaves. All night, our daughters chase crickets.

XI. *A Story*

He said, *This used to be a waterpark*, pointing above
to a car dealership, before listing names of slides.
I only saw neon numbers across windshields; balloons
bobbing with a breeze. June grass resisting the weight of me.
I said, *Your favorite ride?* —*Never went*, he answered,
too expensive, which is probably why they closed it.
He laughed, but didn't stop pointing, didn't stop
naming. Miles away,
                      storm clouds gathered, creating,
in the sky, the look of dark clothes in a heap. I couldn't
feel any drops. Not yet. But from this distance, the rain
hung there, pinned against gray. I didn't say anything,
of course, because this was his story now, because he spoke
as if no one were there, or as if he'd vanished
to where I could not follow. And I took no offense.
Barracuda Blaster, Shotgun Falls, he kept going.
The thing is, he said, *we passed this place
on the way to my aunt's. It used to be*

right here. By then, I thought the winds would pick up
and move the storm toward us, then through us
and we'd have to let it. I stood there, pretending
to be ready until I began to believe myself
—lungs like small, husky wings rising
in my chest. Up. Down. Again. Again.

HORSES

I want to write a poem with horses galloping through it
but I don't know much about horses anymore, except that
they *do* gallop, and I'm only reminded of this by a movie
I fell asleep watching.

           When I was a boy, I'd watch
through a fence as horses shook their manes and galloped
around the ranch next to where my grandfather lived. Perhaps
that part about galloping isn't true. I follow my imagination
more than I should, at least far enough to end this poem with
a charge of horses departing in a cloud of dust or however it is
they vanish. Because they do.

           To be honest, my friend
was the one who loved horses. And if I'm going to tell you
everything, I was in love with her. This was years ago,
in college. Isn't that a great way to start a love story?
How would you write it? Would you include the sycamore tree,
sunlight climbing through it? The shade we sat under.
Afternoons, and a campus slowly emptying.

           Maybe all you need
to know is I wanted her and I to work out long after we didn't,
long after we met up, as friends, at a pizzeria near campus,
where we talked about her mother and sister,

and that cousin
who shoveled dirt every morning, timing himself, because
he wanted to be a firefighter. All that reminiscence as a way
of saying: *Look at what bolts around*
inside us.
          I know
this poet who hates when poets use the word *love*
in their poems. She turns the page on the word;
I've seen her do it. But I wonder what she places there
instead. I picture a pothole, its open gaze crushed clean
by rainwater and tires. I picture a parade of silver fillings,
the mouth waiting to snap something in two.
                        I was listening
to this podcast the other day where a poet explained
how hard it is to write love poems. *The problem is,*
he said, *there's no tension in the love I have for my wife.*
In my headphones, I heard the interviewer exhale
and recognized the ache it floated from. It was a horse
galloping over a hill. There was a pause. The poet said
he might never write a love poem again, if all goes well.
I laughed in my kitchen. I'd been washing dishes. My wife
was getting ready for work. In the background, the clink
of silverware. They were in a restaurant. I couldn't tell
a fork from a spoon, and that bothered me. I listened
for a clatter of neighboring tables. The poet's words
slipped into a whisper behind everything. Sounds of metal
washed over the interview.
                  And isn't love like that?—a shift
of attention the heart demands, a refocusing.
                        I think

the poet I know would be proud of this poem, how it
advances through the tall grass by itself, how it refuses
to sunset. Sometimes,

                    leaving doesn't mean anything
besides ember fading under earth.

                              Another window
in my house is broken. This time,

                         it's the bedroom. Our
neighbor, this kid, has trouble learning when to let go
of a baseball. After the shatter, I found a jagged hole
and stuck my hand through. I waved him away.

                                        Later,
I covered the frame with plastic and told myself I'd fix it
in the summer. It's October now and it keeps the cold out.
The plastic sheet doesn't bother me except at night
when a wind traffics through town, and my ear bends
toward the window's new breath.

                         Tonight,
my wife snores, and I am awake. I press my palm
to the blurred window. Beyond, someone dreams of smoke
and salvation. I know this. I move closer, watch for clouds
grazing in the prayer field, and maybe I ask for nothing at all.

ACKNOWLEDGMENTS, THANK-YOUS, AND SHOUT-OUTS

I want to thank the editors of the literary spaces that first published the following poems, some in their earlier versions and under different names:

BOAAT: "Visits" (published as "Visitations")
Copper Nickel: "Elegy with Puppet Strings"
cream city review: "The Flame"
Forklift, Ohio: "Elegy with Roll Call"
The Georgia Review: "Hired as Professional Mourner at Funeral"
Green Mountains Review: "[Mexican] America" and "[White] America" (published as "[ ] America")
Hot Metal Bridge: "Suspended from School, the Pachuco's Grandson Watches *Happy Days* While His Homie Fulfills Prophecy"
Huizache: "Learning to Box"
Juked: "Down" (in its entirety)
The McNeese Review: "My Neighbor Who Keeps the Dying Things," "1991" (published as "Rumination #7"), and "The Pachuco's Grandson Considers Skipping School"
MIRAMAR: "Horses"

The Missouri Review (Online as Poem of the Week):
"All-American Mexican" (published as "Here's a small
story about the sky . . . ")

The Offing: "Doing Donuts in an '87 Mustang 5.0, after My
Homie Chris Gets Broken Up With" and "All-American
Mexican" (published as "I don't know if I made these
knuckles . . . ")

Okey-Panky: "Push"

Ploughshares: "From My Classroom Window at the Prison,
before Students Arrive"

Poetry: "Because My Brother Knows Why It's Called *County
Blues*, but Won't Tell Me" and "My Brother Is Asking for
Stamps"

Poetry Northwest: "Ars Poetica"

SALT: "Clothespins"

Sixth Finch: "Stop Looking at My Last Name Like That"

Southern Indiana Review: "Teaching at the Prison in
December" (published as "December at Faribault Prison")

Sycamore Review: "The Pachuco's Grandson Considers the
Silversun Pickups' Album Diana Lent Him When They Last
Spoke Seven Years Ago"

Tahoma Literary Review: "The Pachuco's Grandson Smokes
His First Cigarette after Contemplating Masculinity"

Tinderbox Poetry Journal: "My Hometown as a Man Riding
a Bicycle with No Chain"

Water~Stone Review: "After the Man Who Found Me Doing
Burpees at the Park Said: 'I Can Tell You Learned Those
on the Inside.'" and "The Very Short Story of Your Knuckles"

"Minutes, at the Health Clinic" (published as "Minutes") was
included in the chapbook . . . *because not all the times were
great but they were all mine* as part of a chapbook compi-
lation, published by San Gabriel Valley Literary Festival, 2013.

"On Being REMEK" was published in the *Boiler Journal* as their Flash Essay Contest winner, 2015.

"All-American Mexican" (published as "All I wanted was a Cadillac . . . ") was a finalist for the Auburn Witness Poetry Prize and was published by *Southern Humanities Review*.

"After José Clemente Orozco's *Man of Fire*" was published as part of *The Brillantina Project*, created to honor the forty-nine victims of the Orlando tragedy.

I've had the great fortune of living a life filled with the love and generosity of family, friends, homies, and comrades in the arts. I hold a tremendous amount of gratitude for you all.

Thank you, Raquel Salas Rivera, for selecting my manuscript, for believing in my work, for seeing it in this world.

Thank you to Beth Dial and everyone at the National Poetry Series for the important work you all do.

Thank you to Helene Atwan, Liv Bauer, Michelle Betters, Jennifer Canela, Haley Lynch, Melissa Nasson, Susan Lumenello, Sanj Kharbanda, and the entire Beacon Press team for making this real.

I want to thank God. Thank you to my mother and father, Benita and Juan Torres. You both made great sacrifices for all of us. Rose, thank you for reciting Dickinson and encouraging me to gaze at the stars. Lisa, for modeling strength and perseverance. Garr, for teaching me how important it is to laugh and dance. Victor, for being there when I needed it. Debbie and Juan, for your guidance through the years. Marty, for some realness. Tina and Roberto, thank you for making space for the family to gather. Tía Lena, thank you for your constant support. I carry the memory of Cathy with me. Thank you to the tíos y tías, all the cousins of the Torres/z and Terrones clans who've been there for me.

Thank you to very early mentors, Mrs. Swearingen, Coach Sweeney, and Carlos Rodas.

Thank you, Mt. San Antonio College (and associated) mentors/friends: John and Ann Brantingham, Cynthia Prochaska, Michelle Dougherty, Maria Estrada, Kimberly Quintana-Mullane, Bruce Williams (RIP), and Lloyd Aquino. I am forever grateful to you all for encouraging my curiosity. Shaymaa, thank you for inviting me to my first Creative Writing Club meeting. It changed everything. Thank you to Monica, Scott, Elder, Donna Hilbert, Rachel, and Sam for your friendship then and now. To AJ, Michaelsun, and Charlotte: thank you for being wonderful friends and comrades in the arts, from the jump.

Thank you to Robert Chavez, for the laptop—that belief in me meant a lot.

Shout-out to *A Mic and Dim Lights*—especially Cory "Besskepp" Cofer, JB, Kristina Mejia, Matt Sedillo, and David Romero—where I found my first open mic community.

Thank you to UC-Riverside profs/mentors Christopher Buckley, Juan Felipe Herrera, Chris Abani, Tod Goldberg, Jennifer Nájera, and Tiffany López for providing the tools. Thank you, UCR MFAers who offered mentorship and encouragement: Ángel García, David Campos, Brandon Williams, Courtney Lund, and Greg Emilio. To Samir, Matt, Andrea (and Pati and Brenda and fam), Melisa Garcia, and my AOTP fam: your friendship got me through those years.

Reina, my sister: thank you for being there, for giving me the advice I needed, especially when I didn't want to hear it. Shout-out: Leti, Yesi, Los, Andrea, Jorge, Isaac, Jorge, Lettie, Mo, and the entire VS crew (and associated folks) turned homies. Shout-out to Henry Jimenez, my homie, my photographer, there since day one.

Luiza, I will always be grateful for those late-night hot chocolates at Denny's, back when we were figuring out a way into the lives we wanted through higher ed.

To my comadre Patty. I am blessed to have you as a friend and to be part of your family.

To my comadre Liz, my first friend, my oldest friend. You've been a huge influence on my life. I would not be who I am without you. I hope I make you proud.

Shout-out to the original I RUN STREETS & THE WANTED KINGS crews: DIER, KAON, SIRIS, MASE, RAGE, TEAL, JUKE, MAR, GABS, BASEK, DENS, CLAS, HALO, HALA, JEMS, LILS, SHINE, BLOOM, CHROME, et al. Shout-out Pomona (and extended) fam, then and now: Danny, Jesse, Miguel, Jonny (compa, Prrrr!), Balou, Vela, Bernie, Ramon, Arthur, Willy, Noel, Sammy, Chris, Mike, Augie, Ralphie, Alfred (compa!), Johnathan, Henry: this book is for y'all.

Thank you to the MFA program at Minnesota State University, Mankato, and the professors who mentored me: Richard Robbins, Diana Joseph, Dick Terrell, Geoff Herbach, Candace Black, Roger Sheffer, Robin Becker, and Gwen Westerman. Shout-out to my fellow workshoppers/homies: Dennis, Lina, Brad, Reid, Beth, Max, Ben, Cindy, Eric, Jake, Taylor, Dylan, Melissa, Nic, Tyler, Erin, James, Stephanie, Kate, Sean, Justin, Hop, Olivia, Jordan, Drew, each and every Zach, Lorna, Emily, Michelle, Josh, Claire, Mike, and Peter (!).

Shout-out to all my Twin Cities homies who've given me a home away from home away from home. Special shout-out to Poetry Asylum and the Minnesota Prison Writing Workshop. I love all y'all.

Shout-out to the greater literary fam who've inspired, mentored, and challenged me, folks I've been blessed to build with: Paul Tran, Sreshtha Sen, Dustin Pearson, Michael

Shewmaker, Emily Jungmin Yoon, Sebastián Hasani Páramo,
Natalie Diaz, Peggy Robles, Lupe Mendez, Carl Phillips, Elmaz
Abinader, Jonathan Johnson, Marcus Wicker, Matthew Rohrer,
and Ed Skoog.

Thank you to my comrades in poetry/trusted friends/
homies who, respectively, provided essential feedback for this
manuscript: Jess Server, Jude Nutter, Kate McLam, Anders
Carlson-Wee, Sara Borjas, and Mary Szybist. This book would
not be what it is without each of you. I cannot thank you
enough.

Thank you to the following institutions and programs whose
support made this collection possible: the Loft Literary Center
(special shout-out to the Loft Mentor Series), A Very Small Arts
Fund, 410 Project Mankato, the Minnesota State Arts Board,
the Jerome Foundation, the Camargo Foundation, the Palm
Beach Poetry Festival, the Bread Loaf Writers' Conference,
VONA Voices, CantoMundo, and the National Endowment for
the Arts.

To anyone who's ever read my poems, and to whoever will
encounter my work in the future, I hope it moves you as poetry
has moved me.

Finally, to LISSA LISSA LISSA: I keep thinking about the attic,
your coffeemaker, those mornings. More than writing. More
than I could ever thank you for. I love you.

NOTES

"All-American Mexican" ("I don't know if I made these knuckles . . . ")
    was written after Jose Luis Razo Jr. aka the Harvard Homeboy.
"Hired as Professional Mourner at Funeral" was inspired by Philip
    Levine's "My Father with Cigarette Twelve Years before the Nazis
    Could Break His Heart."
"The Flame" was inspired, in part, by my mentor Dick Terrill and also by
    Terrance Hayes's poem "The Deer."
"Learning to Box" is dedicated to Miguel Garcia and his brothers.
Both "[Mexican] America" and "[White] America" were written after
    Allen Ginsberg and Danez Smith.
"Down" (as a whole) has several points of inspiration: Frank Stanford's
    What About This; "In Defense of Small Towns," by Oliver de la Paz;
    "I Go Back to Berryman's," by Vincent Scarpa; Kendrick Lamar's
    "The Art of Peer Pressure"; and a Good Thunder Reading Series
    Workshop led by Diana Spechler, 2016.
"Clothespins" was inspired by my friend and mentor Christopher
    Buckley and his poem "Getting There."
"Push" was inspired, in part, by the first line in "The Crimes of the
    Shade Trees," by Larry Levis.
"The Very Short Story of Your Knuckles" was inspired by the "Gospel"
    poem series in Tracy K. Smith's *The Body's Question*.
"The Pachuco's Grandson Considers Skipping School" is dedicated to
    my homie Jesse Rodriguez.
"All-American Mexican" ("Here's a small story about the sky . . .")
    was inspired by Alberto Ríos's poem "A Small Story about the Sky."

"Suspended from School, the Pachuco's Grandson Watches *Happy Days* While His Homie Fulfills Prophecy" was inspired by Sonia Sanchez's "Norma."

"After the Man Who Found Me Doing Burpees at the Park Said: 'I Can Tell You Learned Those on the Inside.'" was written after a Good Thunder Reading Series workshop led by Marcus Wicker, 2017.

"Ars Poetica" is dedicated to Mayra Juarez, who provided the photograph on which this poem is based.

"My Neighbor Who Keeps the Dying Things" was written after a conversation with my friend Dennis Scott Herbert.

"Elegy with Puppet Strings" was inspired by Milan Kundera's *Festival of Insignificance* and Alberto Ríos's "Domingo Limón" and is dedicated to Ricardo Juarez.

The entire "Pachuco's Grandson" series was heavily influenced by my CantoMundo fellowship, in particular my first retreat in Austin, Texas, 2016.

"All-American Mexican" ("All I wanted was a Cadillac . . . ") was inspired, in part, by Dennis Scott Herbert's fiction piece "Not Like This: Recollections from the Sustainment Chamber."

"Elegy with Roll Call" was inspired by dear friends of mine, Ben Cisewski and Luiza Gallardo. The line "The further away/ I am, the harder I look for home" in the "Confession" section is a variation of a line in Alberto Ríos's poem "The Fall of the Bears."

The "All-American Mexican" series was heavily influenced by Gloria E. Anzaldúa's *Borderlands/La Frontera: The New Mestiza* and Angelica Maria Barraza's *Dreams the Water Gave Me*.